CONTINUOUS PERFORMANCE

Poems by Maggie Jaffe

VIET NAM GENERATION, INC.
&
BURNING CITIES PRESS

Viet Nam Generation, Inc. & Burning Cities Press
2921 Terrace Drive, Chevy Chase, Maryland 20815
ISBN: 0-96285424-6-5

Cover illustration: *Allegory of America*, Cornelis Visscher, Dutch engraver, 16th century, courtesy of the New York Historical Society.

An asterisk in the text refers to the "Notes" page.

With special thanks to Kali Tal, Mary Williams
& Jim McMenamin.

Grateful acknowledgement is made to the following
journals in which these poems first appeared:

"America," *G.W. Review.*
"Thomas Morton" and "Hawthorne's Letter A," *Bakunin.*
"Custer's Nomenclature," *Anaconda Press.*
"Emily Dickinson" and "The Old God of War," *Visions.*
"Melville," *Without Halos.*
"Heinrich Heine" and "Oppie," *Free Lunch.*
"Long White Train," *sub-TERRAIN.*
"In Alamogordo," *Red Dirt.*
"Guatemala: Your Jewel," *Telegraphy.*
"Death of Che," *Vol. No.*
"Ernesto Cardenal," "Robert Earl Mack," "Up An' Atom," "New
[World] Ordure," "In Dark Times," *San Fernando
        Poetry Journal.*
"Tarzan," "Hanoi, Jane?," "Frida Kahlo," "Imelda Marcos,"
        Portable Wall.
"In A San Diego Sweat," *Sing Heavenly Muse!.*
"Bertolt Brecht," and "Evita Peron," *Santa Monica Review.*
"Information Explosion," *Gypsy.*
"At The Writer's Colony" and "Murder, Inc.," *Bouillabaisse.*
"The Girls of Glasnost," *Left Curve.*
"Magic Realism," *The Echo Room.*
"Custer's Last Laugh," "Maria Callas," "Patrice Lumumba,"
"Ascetic Revolutionary," *Viet Nam Generation.*
"In The Distinguished Liberal," *The Women's Review of
        Books.*
"For E.M., County Cork," *Americas Review.*
"Paul Robeson," *The Vincent Brothers Review.*
"George Grosz," "Gustav Mahler," "Like Edgar Allen Poe," "Luz
        Parra," "Murder, Inc.," "At the Unemployment Office,"
        Chiron Review

For Harold, rescuer of injured birds,

and for my parents

Contents

America

In the 16th century
Allegory of America,
America's a "tawny-hued savage,"
nearly naked, full hipped,
breasty, straddling a fantastic
creature, part armadillo, part boar.
In the 18th century
America's renamed Columbia,
personifying Discovery.
Less than a hundred
years later, Columbia
metamorphoses into
Liberty,
symbolizing Freedom
[to make money
contingent on indigenous removal].
In 1886, the same year that Liberty's
installed in New York Harbor,
Geronimo surrenders to
the United States
government.
At Her stone feet,
cracked mollusk shells
once used as wampum.

Thomas Morton

prefers to dance round
the Maypole with savage
women & rude boys
dressed in bear
skins, antelope horns.
Morton also loves to fuck,
with or without the king's consent,
which is why he is devil kin.
Mostly he rails against money,
displeasing the Puritan Fathers.
As penance, they chain him
to the stocks, burn down
Merry Mount, then,
for good measure,
genocide the Pequots.*
Thereafter, they raze
the land, laying the
foundation for civilized
prisons, banks, nursing
homes, copying centers,
think tanks . . .

[for Richard Drinnon]

Custer's Nomenclature

*"My voice is for war!"**

The Kiowa called him
Creeping Panther.
White Man Runs Him
gave Custer his own sacred moniker:
Son Of Morning Star.
Custer's men called him
Hard Ass, Iron Butt, Ringlets.
For Libby, his wife,
he was her Little Boy.
"Shoot Libby in the head
if she's captured," he ordered.
"You know what they do
to white women."
He dubbed his Indian
mistress Sunshine.
But White Bull was the last to name him:
"Now Long Hair lies at my feet."
If not for the plot to assassinate
Lincoln or his own death,
Custer was scum enough
to be president.
A blood-red arrow would have
traced his weird trajectory:
West Point, Wild West,
Wall Street, White House.

Custer's Last Laugh
[for Leonard Peltier]

Dateline: Cheyenne, Montana, July 4, 1992.
According to the *L.A.Times*
Indian activists misspelled
key words in their own
commemorative plaque
for warriors who fought
The Battle of Little Big Horn.
While wedded to grammar
but committed to amnesia,
The *Times* reports [page 24]
the plaque's misspelling of "Cavalry"
so it reads "Calvary."
There are other technical
errors as well . . .
The *Times* won't divulge how
Custer's 7th Cavalry
searched & destroyed their elderly
pacified their women and children
terminated their horses
wasted their buffalo to starve them.

*"Language is the perfect
instrument of Empire."* *

Emily Dickinson

One of the few women
you can trust to keep
her mouth shut.
Dressed in virgin white,
married to Imagination.
Writing of ruby-throated
hummingbirds, Sir Death,
exquisite states of being.
Close by, Abolitionists thunder
out their oratory—
from the pulpit,
on street corners,
from the marriage bed,
from Frederick Douglass's
Prison House of Slavery—
even from her Papa's parlor.
But good girls won't disrupt
the class
for Lit profs who teach
the air-brushed canon:
15 [dead] white men & Emily.
Shoot the canon!

[for Deborah Small]

Melville

*"I stand for the heart.
To the dogs with the head."*
—from a letter to Hawthorne

In the British edition of *Typee,
Or A Peep At Polynesian Life,*
he writes: "The civilized
white man is the most
ferocious animal on the
face of the earth."
Though these polemics
were deleted from
the American edition,
his reviewers still
slaughtered him.
At 12, he's penniless;
by 19 he ships out:
a working stiff,
"dollars damned" him.
Later, in the Custom House,
weighing in Imperial spoils,
Billy Budd wedged in his desk
like dirty postcards men
bring home from foreign ports.
His "failure" as a writer
nearly cost him his sanity.

Hawthorne's Letter A

John Hathorne* took up
his bible & the law: 20 women
condemned to death for
adultery, incest, witchery.
Sins of Fathers indeed
weigh on their Progeny.
Nonetheless, Hawthorne was soft
on slavery but hard on Melville
whose hard-on for him is legendary:
all that Melvillean heave & gush.
Within Empire's thrust,
Hawthorne might be an introverted writer
but that don't make him a woman.
His "real" friends are Longfellow
& "tedious, intolerable" Thoreau.
Sofia, his wife, the first
to read *The Scarlet Letter*
prompting an excruciating migraine.
He notes: "This book is my triumph!"
In truth, is Hester's A for Adultery,
or for the more heinous stain of Incest—
scourge of our best families?
Busybody Lit crits want to know.

Tarzan

fears race mixing,
not only with *Wogs*
but with *Apes* who raised him.
In truth, he's an Englishman
from the jolly good mother country,
who innately knows the value of private
property & Darwinian hierarchies.
By his own account,
"killer of beasts and blacks."
Tarzan's the romantic image
of Edgar Rice Burroughs himself.
Burroughs, like Custer before him,
joined the Hostile-slaughtering 7th
Cavalry when *dead Hostiles*
metamorphosed into *Noble Savages.*
Custer too lived by the pen & sword:
his student-essay, "The Red Man,"
justified Indian genocide.
He's better known, though,
for *My Life On The Plains,*
an *Aryan* romance,
similar in genre, if not in style,
to *Tarzan of the Apes.*

Like Edgar Allan Poe

Anastasio Somoza attended West Point
only 50 years later. Both learned the art
of Empire building. Yet Poe is
expelled for boozing & gambling,
not for being a pro-slaver.
In the end, Dixie, where he's dragged
from one polling place to another,
earning drinks for each dead
man's vote. Until he collapses,
implodes, damn near explodes
at Ryan's 4th Ward, 1849.
He's buried alive in a Baltimore cemetery!
He should be so lucky.
Poe's buried in an unmarked
pauper's grave.

Take Somoza: he can fuck grown women
& hold his liquor. Not puke during torture.
Somoza & Sons never lost an election.*
Not with Presidents **Roosevelt**, **Truman**,
Eisenhower, *Kennedy*, **Johnson**, **Nixon**,
Ford & **CARTER** in their corner.

Heinrich Heine

"Religion mixes sweet tranquilizing drops,
like a spiritual opiate, into the bitter cup
of humanity."
—from a letter to Marx

All he *really* wanted
was the sexual
abandon of the *goyim.*
Hence his embrace of morphine
and the Catholic Church.
In spite of conversion
his esteemed *goyim*
Jew-baited his worked-over poetry.
Nonetheless he loves and hates
his *Deutschland über alles.*
He thinks: maybe I should
emigrate to *Amerika*
"that Freedom Stable where
all the boors live equally."
It's 1825: Heine knows what
they do there to the *Schwarze.*
Chooses Paris instead
where he writes lyrical
poems about Germany
and a political analysis
of the *Can-Can.*
Heine said:
"People who burn books
will also burn people."

Oppie

can't sleep
desert heat.
Reads Donne's
"Batter my heart
three-personed God."
Names the first atomic
bomb, *Trinity.*
Still, he's suspect:
"Jewboy, comm'nist,
faggot," barks
J. Edgar Hoover,
of all people.
The desert's nothing
like D.C. or New York.
Here cowboys talk with
marbles in their mouths.
And girls who work the all-night
diners chew gum with
the single-minded
intensity of Science.
One day the girls will head
out west, metamorphosing
into Hollywood bombshells.
Then Oppie'll have to make
his own damn coffee
with regrets about *Gilda,*
detonated over Bikini,
without his consent.

In Alamogordo

intense heat & flash
explode the night
with too much light!
like the flesh-
eating second sun
prophesied in legends . . .
Later Laguna Pueblos
cut radiated wood
for their houses.
Children born with
"mad white cells"
nearly double.
Painful inflammation
in joints and muscles.
Combing hair out
in the morning sink,
Science scalps the
Scalpers.

"Up An' Atom"

After radiating their top soil
a "half-life" of 50,000 years
the army's in a quandary,
though they insist "we have a plan."
Force-move the population
to a reservation.
People told to "wait it out."
Cheerful as children,
Bikinians sing in Marshallese,
"You are my sunshine,
my only sunshine.
You make me happy
when skies are blue . . . ."
The fuck we do.
After 23 detonations
we finally sank two atolls
[which was not our objective].
Then the army tells us:
"terminate testing."
Am I blue?
Since then, nothing's right.
My hands & feet
swole up & cracked.
I'm queasy all the damn
time, especially mornings,
like I was pregnant.

Long White Train

Woke up this moanin' *blues*.
Long white train
carrying atomic waste
through the heart-
land *blues*.
Uranium/Plutonium lung
cancer *blues*.
Long time gone *blues*.
Made for TV Nazi/Skinhead *blues*.
Black brother drowning
in his vomit *blues*.
Starving pregnant Chicana *blues*.
Red, White, & Blue *blues*.
So proudly we heil *blues*.
By the bomb's early light *blues*.
Reagan/Bush selling off the
"wilderness" *blues*.
Reservation suicide *blues*.
Unless you bury the shit on your
ancestors if you wanna live *blues*.

Evita Perón

In Argentina
"Indians are like grass,"
while the pampas stretch to infinity,
and everything's up for grabs.
From the slums to the pink
Presidential Palace,
her fire-red lips
the envy of Buenos Aires,
with a whore's expertise
for giving head.
Onassis paid ten
thousand dollars for one
night alone with her.
When she died of uterine cancer
at 33, the press detailed
her French lingerie
on her emaciated corpse.
The Church chastised her vanity.
Her enemies "disappeared" magically.
She had the Oligarchy by the balls.
Which is why her *Pobrecitos*
loved it when she asked:
"Shall we burn down *El Barrio Norte*
where those rich sons-of-bitches live?"

Maria Callas

Dark eyed, bird-like,
she made herself
svelte.
Her crystal voice
needed constant honing.
Audiences loved how
she suffered for Art.
She loved a billionaire
who instead married Jackie K.
For publicity? for kinky sex?
In Pasolini's *Medea*,
her last performance,
she wouldn't sing
but she's riveting
as the beautiful, tragic
infanticide.
Pharmaceuticals and
booze destroyed her voice.
She died in Paris alone.
Well, her maid was with her.

Imelda Marcos

No more stale jokes
about her sixteen hundred
pairs of shoes.
Sure she laundered
money but never asked
anyone to kiss her [ass]ets.
Though charges against her
are dropped, exile's rough.
At the Maui Hilton, barefoot
& lonely as Friday, Imelda's
too bummed to shop.

Blame it on Manifest Destiny
"which swept these magnificent
Aryans across the Pacific,"
bringing light to "goo-goos,
niggers & their squaws."
The bodies stacked up like shoes.
Black soldiers deserted in droves:
never could cotton to water torture.
Still, William James, speaking for
the Anti-imperialist League,
had [for what it's worth] the last word:
*God damn the U.S. for its vile
conduct in the Philippines.*"
And god damn the Marcos-acquitting courts.

Paul Robeson

played football
but wouldn't play hard ball
with whitey.
He loved beautiful women.
Loved beautiful [white] women,
which is illegal.
He was red & Black,
way too hot for the '50s.
In D.C., Hollywood,
Peekskill, New York,
they nearly lynched him.
At his career's height,
the FBI took away his pass
port.
On his deathbed he insisted
the CIA tried to poison him—
not in Mississippi or Alabama
but at a party in "godless"
Russia, for god's sake.

Patrice Lumumba

Joseph Conrad sailed up the Congo
on the *Roi des Belges* while King
Leopold ordered *Black* workers
mutilated if they didn't feed
ivory quotas to their Masters.
By the time Leopold founded the
Association for Civilization
in Central Africa, the dead
exceeded eleven million.
What Conrad really saw we'll
never know except as *shadows*,
ghosts, the *metaphysical*
heart's darkness.
We do know he didn't see
the *practical* policy
of colonization.
Sixty years later Lumumba's
life cut short by Belgian
mercenaries and the CIA.
Where did his butchers stuff him?

Bertolt Brecht

fled Hitler's Germany
for McCarthy's *Amerika*
where he'll bomb on Broadway,
go hungry in Hollywood.
Only HUAC understood his work.
They accused him
of "premature anti-fascism."
He denied everything.
They believed him.
"Americans aren't as bad
as Nazis. At least they let you
smoke while they interrogate you,"
Brecht said smoking his cigar.
Besides cigars, he loved
brainy women with red
radical politics.
An irascible, rumpled-looking
foreigner in the Halls of Justice,
hating the Jew-
hater and the big
boss man, he wrote:
*"What is the crime
of robbing a bank
compared with
the crime
of founding one."*

Georg Grosz
"Art is Shit!"

So are the bourgeoisie
who crave the Shock of the New!
but hate Revolution, 1919.
Grosz's "art is a weapon"
against the Ruling Class.
Yet he paints women
rapacious naked pink:
working girls in cahoots
with Capital, not *workers*.
Which is why he's
"the saddest man in Europe,
a phenomenon of grief."
A small *no* in the big
YES! of Nazi Germany . . .
Escapes to America
where he's mostly ignored
by the upbeat, happy *Volk*,
but not by HUAC.
Back in *Deutschland*,
will never again work
for The Party.
While partying, he falls
down drunk & dies.
Grosz's heart stopped in '59.

Gustav Mahler

"The talented little Jew?"
hissed Cosima Wagner,
Liszt's bastard daughter.
Not even his pledge to the *Volk*
will assuage her.*
In his longed-for-death
dream, there is blessed silence.
Like God, Mahler must fill
the void with *his* sound.
He wakes to morning cacophony:
birdsquawk, screaming brats, un-
faithful Alma . . . usual gnawing doubts.
Later he converts.
Soon after he dies of heart failure.
Mahler won't play his beloved
Wagner for the monsters in
Auschwitz, Belsen, Dachau.
Still, in the Occupied Territories, Mahler,
not Wagner, might be played
during "routine" interrogation.

[for the '67 Green Line]

Walter Benjamin

dreamt of a labyrinth-
like bookstore and was happy.
Then woke in Vichy, France—
Autumn, 1940.
Frankly, he's unlucky—
more dreamer than schemer,
equating scheming with Capital.
Which is why he's at this sealed-
off border, crossing into the only
country which will have him.
His suicide "so profoundly moved
the guards," they allowed his
comrades passage into Spain,
god damn them.
Were his books with his
"unintelligible marginalia"
beside him?
Unintelligible to whom?

Self alienation

has reached
a point that it
experiences its own
destruction as
aesthetic pleasure.

Fascism

aestheticizes
politics
which culminates
in one thing:

War.

Frida Kahlo

"*Pain is yellow-green,*"
nuns click on & off,
gringo doctors calculate.
Sharp white walls devoid
of color. She'll paint grey-
green monkeys, reddish-
purple hummingbirds,
like "ancient Aztec blood."
Whom & what did she love?
Cigarettes, "*cocktailitos,*"
women, children & Diego
Rivera, her "frog prince."
Her frog prince fucked *gringas,*
actresses, even her sister.
In turn, she screwed with Trotsky,
whom she later denounced:
he was a Trotskyite.
She loathed "*Gringolandia,*" the color
yellow, *Yanqui Imperialismo.*
Her last major paintings were
an unfinished portrait of Stalin;
Marxism Gives Health to the Sick;
& *Viva La Vida,* dedicated to Mexico.
At 47 years old she'll die of a
complicated leg amputation.
At her grave, Diego—"haggard & grey"—
became an old man in a matter of hours.

Death Of Che

On the day that
Che Guevara died
a woman, thirtyish,
from the wealthy
"first circle" of La Paz,
exploded her heart with a
snub-nosed .38. Radios played
Morir por Amor/to die for love.
Even his executioner,
Barrientos, that shit,
felt a "great loss"
at his dying.
Che was betrayed
by the CIA
and Bolivian peasants
he meant to aid,
wanted to love.
Che said: "I can't sleep
on a mattress while my soldiers
are shivering up there."
And he divided men into two groups:
those who can sleep
on a mattress
while others suffer
& those who won't.

In The Distinguished Liberal

newspaper
I read of the Salvadoran poet
now living in Nicaragua
who came here to speak
of her country (Neruda's
"delicate waist of America")
of the rich volcanic earth
of *corona de cristo* that blooms blood red
of executions in the dark /
dark cages filled with the dying
of "white hands" smeared
on their victim's walls.
The distinguished liberal
newspaper headlined its story
"Salvadoran Misery." Of course
severed heads are a misery.
Mutilated Indians are a misery.
Military escalations promoted
as humanitarian aid are a misery.
Yet *she* speaks of revolution
in San Salvadoran factories
in liberation churches
in pueblo-owned *milpas*
after monsoon when the sweet
green corn ripens.

[for Claribel Alegría]

Guatemala: Your Jewel

Sun on corrugated iron,
on broken down adobes.
Smell of grilled tortillas,
market women whispering.
Twelve men were taken,
among them the village
healer. Forced in the trunk
of a late-model Pontiac.
Smashed in his face so that
no one could claim him.
A committee is scheduled to investigate.
Who is left? Two small boys,
one scrawny goat, his pregnant
wife. Her life's used up like
the Resplendent quetzal,
extinct almost, once "the jewel
of the highland jungles."
What is left? A large debt owed
to the coffee *finquero*
who in turn owes *quetzales*
to *Banco de Guatemala*
who in turn owes dollars
to Bank America
who in turn owes capital
to Coca-Cola.

Ernesto Cardenal

defies the modernist
truism that
"poetry makes nothing happen."
At a rally of fascists,
disguised as Americans,
who want to "Light Up The Border,"
who want us to all speak *Ingles,*
I spoke out loud a line from your poem:
"The earth belongs to everyone,
not just the rich!"
Along with "the people united
will never be defeated," we yelled
to the [Klans]man in his Mercedes,
to the family in their Ford,
to cops with snarling dogs,
to Mexican-Americans who accused
us of being *Los Communistas:*
"The earth belongs to everyone,
not just the rich!"

San Diego/Tijuana, 1990

Hanoi, Jane?

"Some of the best people in Amerika
today are behind bars."
     —Jane Fonda, 1968

Like Hera, Zeus' consort,
she's everywhere:
on videos, cassettes, CDs.
At ball games, parades,
doing the Tomahawk Chop
& the Persian Gulf Rag.
Living high on the hog
in Georgia, known for its juicy
peaches & electric chair,
"affectionately" called
Yellow Mama.
Still she pisses people off.
Beautiful women should be spread,
not heard, according to Jimmy
Swaggart & a recent Gallup Poll
conducted by CNN news
& the Heritage Foundation.
She *is* annoying.
Hollywood High,
followed by Finishing School.
Her father's good looks,
her silicone boobs,
her unbearably shrill voice,
in spite of elocution lessons.

Duke Wayne

"Please God, don't let us have killed John Wayne."*

Who dispatched more Hostiles than
TB & Winchester repeating rifles.
Rode deep into **Marlboro Country**
for Trinity, a bar girl he knew
from Alamogordo.
Hightailed it back to **Disney**
along the Santa Ana Freeway.
This here's no Hollywood
cowboy, he's been to Viet Nam.
Who yelled *Westward, Ho!* in B-52s.
Rode shotgun out of Saigon
with the Dead End Kids.
Refused their sunshine,
smack & reefer.
Bring me the scalp
of gook/dink/slope,
he said in his fat ass
Texas drawl.
Who's immortalized in Orange
County, shell of the once-great
defense industry.
Given the kiss of death
by fairy computer
programmers, Sixties leftists,
insist the Duke's most loyal fans.

For E.M., County Cork

"That bullshit about
god, country, freedom's
just that." Special Forces,
Da Nang: legs blown. Right eye
cupped delicately in pocket,
slow crawl through rain-
soaked paddies, purple haze.
Later breakup in the States.
Blew it once in Connecticut
woods: fall leaves blaze
up like napalm; rabbits
freeze in shotgun sights
of high school boys
dying to men.
In Cork, then, he chain
smokes Marlboros [reefer
alternated with Guinness-is-good-
for-you, occasionally codeine].
Sits immobile as an ancient priest
who reads his country's
entrails from last week's
Time magazine—
For a man with his life
on his hands, it's a blessing
to be surrounded by ancestors.
Besides, being crippled in Ireland
isn't all that unusual.

Ascetic Revolutionary

Gaunt, humorless, laconic.
Will pick your pocket
for the revolution.
Leaflets the funky movie
house on the eve of war,
January 15, 1991.
The flick is *Berkeley in the Sixties.*
Like prisoners of war
from the last 20 years of yuppie
bullshit, he shows us photos from *his*
revolutionary outpost in Peru.
Contact with *Sendero Luminoso?** I ask.
Yeah, he says, it's wild.
And I know that he's lying.
The system sticks in his throat
like a jammed M-16
or *your* stolen credit card
or a "smart" bomb
graffitied with "Daffy Duck
was Here!"

At The Writer's Colony

What's put under erasure:
writings by "~~Colored Others.~~"
What's privileged: "workshopping," craft.
Stories your kids could eat:
they're wholesome as Disney,
self-censored as the Helms'
Commission on art & pornography,
uncritical of Empire as TV.

At the adjacent supermarket,
someone's dad glares at my husband,
a dead ringer for Fidel's kid brother.
Author of *Guerrilla Writing*,
he's got the look which says
¡No, in thunder!
In line behind us, a student,
white male, wears *the* T-shirt
of Che with sheepish bravado.

Abscess, seepage, rupture
"inside the monster."*
Liberate the lobsters!
Expropriate the best sellers!
Shoot *The New Yorker* in the kneecaps!
Interrogate the whole damn magazine rack!

In A San Diego Sweat

shop
wedged between massage/
tattoo parlors
Chinese women sew
piece work.

At their bone-tired
feet, "camo" cloth
become uniforms—
become soldiers slain
on alien fields—
become money in the bank,
that you can bank on.

For luck & prosperity,
a red wax Buddha lights
up the shop's dark corner.

For lunch: rice with
shrimp speared on chop-
sticks, gaudy and plastic.

I think of red-crowned
cranes *(Grus antigona)*
hunched up in chemical waste.

Robert Earl Mack

42, laid off, charged with murder
of Michael Konz, 25, a "human
relations counselor,"
hired by General Dynamics
to represent them against labor.
Mack has 24 years on the line
assembling Tomahawk
Cruise Missiles
in sunny San Diego, voted
"America's Finest"
by the City Fathers.
Mack's lawyer will offer
an insanity plea.
If found sane during the shootout,
Mack, who is black, *who is black,*
will fry a lighter shade of grey,
though Amnesty International
calls the electric chair,
"barbaric."
Mack, his eyes "bulging
like golf balls," according to
the *L.A. Times*, said:
"They just stole 25 years
of my life. What was I supposed to do?"

Luz Parra

cleans bathrooms at the heavily
endowed [by whom?] university
for more than minimum wage
but no benefits.
For 3 years Luz has been
a "Temp." If she has any
complaints she must first see
one of five "Directors of Management."
Lately they've gotten on her
for not speaking English:
but drudgery is its own universal language.
When her "position is terminated,"
she tells one director:
"I have two kids and no husband."
"That's not my problem," he answers.
Luz carries glowing
letters of recommendation
from students & professors to the
Employment Development Department,
an upbeat euphemism
for the Unemployment Office,
"because language is also polluted.
The defoliation of El Salvador
is a 'Resource Control Program,'
but it's also the defoliation of language.
*And language avenges itself to communicate."**

At The Unemployment Office
[after Wislawa Szymborska]

"It's the welfare chiselers."
"I want to work, so I lay down until
    the feeling passes."
"I told him, 'Join the Marines, they'll
    make you a man.'"
"I got laid off in Jersey, and it's the
    same crap here."
"She asked me if I had a problem
    with serving drinks
in a bikini and high heels."
"We moved back here from Oregon.
You think it's bad here, you should
    see it there."
"I'm voting for Ross Perot.
He understands the working man."
"My husband makes good money.
Well, maybe not that good."
"We're lucky not to be living in Russia."

The Girls Of Glasnost

Not revolutionary workers
in overalls or jeans
but beauty pageant contestants:
titski, asski equals doughski
made in Americki
marketed by at&t,
abc, t.i.t.:
the brave new
Multinational
Corp.
On Red Square,
any given night,
a thousand points of blue
mesmerizing lights:
Dallas, MTV, The Price is Right.
The Girls think America's
"fantastic!"
they've seen it on TV:
"both miracle and weapon
because it shows unfree people
exactly what they're missing."*

Hacker

[for Katya Komisaruk, given 5 yrs for hacking
up the Navy's computer with an ax]

Not your Sixties
hippy-dippy anti-tech,
but a new breed:
whitemale, 25, computer
science major, suburban
mall shopper, church goer.
Can access anything:
NASA, Bank of America,
the Pentagon, the Vatican.
Will work for
IBM, TRW, UNISYS
[dreadful in South Africa].

Replicating, self-
destructing viruses
have been planted into
military computers.
According to *Time*
the culprits are "techno-nerds
with primitive social skills
and a startling indifference
to personal hygiene."
Your hacker does *not,* we repeat,
care a fig for peace.

Magic Realism

She's a minor union functionary.
For weeks she and her co-unionists
have negotiated with the government
to set a minimum working wage for children.
Her file is directed to appropriate channels.
The White Hand *[Las Manos Blancas]*,
funded by the government,
break into her house, decapitate
her five children, seat
them around the kitchen table.
One soldier drives a nail through
the youngest child's head
to keep it from slipping.
In the barracks that night
soldiers watch their favorite TV programs:
The Adventures of Bat Man And Robin,
followed by a local Televangelist,
trained in the USA,
who confirms what everyone knows:
there are murderous
Communistas everywhere.
In El Salvador
dollars magically
make things happen.
Shit happens.

Murder, Inc.

[After Neruda's "United Fruit Co."]

When the trumpets sound
[bite] they call all the tyrants
to themselves:
Barrientos, murderer of Che.
Pinochet, murderer of Allende.
Nixon, murderer of Cambodia, Laos,
the Black Panthers.
Reagan/Bush, murderers of poor
people of color.
When the trumpets sound
[bite] they call all the subsidiaries
who have financed the tyrants to themselves:
AT&T aligned with the CIA in Chile.
McCann Erickson Advertising Agency,
marketing Exxon, Nestle, the San Diego Zoo,
as well as D'Aubuisson & his genocidal Arena Party.
General Electric, makers of ground-to-air missiles,
endorsed by their affiliate, NBC.
Dow Chemical, manufacturers of silicone implants
as well as napalm/phosphorus bombs.
American Cynamid, creators of "Beautiful hair, Breck,"
who offer unemployment or sterilization
to their West Virginia workers.

Information Explosion

She is taken to the "operating theater"
[American Standard].
Stripped, shaved **[Gillette]**.
Injected with drugs to block
endorphins, the body's "natural"
pain suppressor **[Sandoz]**.
Given electric shocks to her gums,
her vagina **[AT&T]**.
Her screams are recorded on a cassette **[Toshiba]**.
Her screams will later be used during her
husband's and children's "sessions."
After their disappearance their names
will be filed under the category
Subversive, Code Red **[IBM]**.
She called it Argentina's institutionalized terrorism,
we call it **Magic of the Marketplace.**

New [World] Ordure

Leon, Nicaragua, a year
before the fall of Somoza
a courthouse facade reads:
GOD   ORDER   JUSTICE
[in that order].
That sonofabitch, Tachito Somoza,
his pleated white shirt
"stained with blood & chili!"

San Juan, Puerto Rico:
the prison fronts Columbus's
statue. Inside, a U.S. Marine kicks
in the teeth of an *Independendista* . . .
Known for discovery but not for slavery,
Columbus brought the wheel & cross,
then used them to torture.

What does the New [World] Order mean?*
Napalm-phosphorus-cluster-fuel air-
percussion-smart bombs.
Ground-to-air missiles
on the White House lawn.
And police. To police the colored
poor into the next century.

The Old God Of War

stands between a rock
and hard place.
He smells of booze and stale cigarettes
and displays his testicles to children.
He's been rejuvenated by professors.
In a hoarse wolfish voice he declares
love for everything young.
A pregnant woman trembles.
He plays the fool and dives for her skirts.
Without shame he presents himself
as a great lover of the **New World Order**
He describes how he put barns
in order by emptying them.
He feeds the poor with bread
he takes from the poor.
His voice, now loud, now soft, is always hoarse.
Loudly he speaks of great times to come.
Softly he teaches women obedience
and how to cook crow.
Meanwhile, he keeps looking
nervously around.
And every five minutes he assures
his delighted public that he'll take
up very little of their time.

["Imitations," Bertolt Brecht, 1938-41]

Suicide Of The Refugee W.B.
[for Walter Benjamin, died 1940]

They said you raised your hand
against yourself
anticipating the butcher's embrace.
After eight years in exile
you closely observed the triumph of the will.
At last, brought against an impassable frontier,
you passed, they say, into the only
country which would have you.

Empires collapse.
Gangsters strut like statesmen.
The people disappear
under an array of elaborate weapons.

The future lies in darkness,
the impulse for righteousness is weak.
All this was too plain to you
when you destroyed a tortured body.

["Imitations," Bertolt Brecht, 1941-47]

In Dark Times

While the impotent house-painter
crushed the workers,
poets wrote about the wind-
shook walnut trees.
While the great wars were prepared for,
they wrote about children skimming
flat stones across the rapids.
While the great powers
joined forces against the workers,
they wrote about a stunning
actress's entrance into rooms
of wealth, "culture," power.
Those who come after
won't say the times were dark,
rather why were the poets silent?

["Imitations," Bertolt Brecht, 1936-38]

Notes

"Thomas Morton": One of the original Puritan settlers in Plymouth, Morton described the Pequots as "godless" but harmonious with their surroundings [*New English Canaan*, 1637]. Governor John Endicott, & other Puritans, likened them to "savages." Correspondingly, Morton perceived the "New World" as an abundant garden, while the Puritans described it as "a wilderness." Selling guns to the Indians was the major pretext for Morton's arrest.

"Custer's Nomenclature": *"My voice is for war"* was the nine-year-old Custer's enthusiastic utterance while witnessing a soldier's parade.

"Custer's Last Laugh": *"Language is the perfect instrument of Empire"* was the reply of Antonio de Nebrija, author of the first *Gramatica* [1492] to Queen Isabella when she asked the importance of a grammar.

"Hawthorne's Letter 𝕬": Hawthorne added a "w" to his name, in part to distance himself from his forefathers.

"Like Edgar Allan Poe": Anastasio [Tacho] Somoza and his son, Tachito, were dictators of Nicaragua for approximately fifty years with support from eight United States presidents. About [Tacho], FDR said: "He's a son-of-a-bitch, but he's our son-of-a-bitch."

"Gustav Mahler": Cosima Wagner opposed Mahler's appointment as Munich Opera Director because of her antisemitism.

"Duke Wayne": *"Please God, don't let us have killed John Wayne"* was overheard at an atomic testing site adjacent to the movie set, *The Conqueror*, Utah, 1956. Forty-one percent of the cast and crew developed cancer, including Susan Hayward, Dick Powell, Agnes Moorhead, Pedro Armendariz, Jeanne Gerson, along with John Wayne.

"Ascetic Revolutionary": *Sendero Luminoso* or The Shining Path [as the "bourgeois press" calls them] are Maoist, Quechua Indians largely comprised of women, who advocate the violent overthrow of government followed by the return to a pre-Columbian society.

"At The Writer's Colony": *Inside the Monster* [1898] is a collection of José Martí's essays critical of the United States' racist/Imperialist policies.

"Luz Parra": The last lines, somewhat modified, are from Ernesto Cardenal, "Epistle to José Coronel Urtecho," *Zero Hour and Other Documentary Poems* (New York: New Directions, 1980).

"The Girls of Glasnost": The last line is from Benjamin Stern, "Ultimate American Weapon," *Los Angeles Times*, March 24, 1990.

"New [World] Ordure": New World Order is an amalgam of Hitler's New Order and Columbus's New World.

Born in New York City in 1948, Maggie Jaffe presently lives in San Diego with the novelist, Harold Jaffe, and their cat, Tosh. For a number of years, they traveled in South & Central America & the Caribbean. Maggie is the author of *The Body Politic;* and with Deborah Small, the co-author of *1492: What Is It Like To Be Discovered?* Her poems are published in numerous journals and anthologies. She teaches at San Diego State University and San Diego City College. She is art editor of *Fiction International.*